When the DEVIL

Makes an

Offer

How to Escape Satan's Plan to Trap You

David B. Smith

Pacific Press® Publishing Association
Nampa, Idaho
Oshawa, Ontario, Canada

Edited by Kenneth R. Wade
Designed by Tim Larson
Cover photo by Hans Neleman/©Image Bank

Copyright © 1997 by
Pacific Press® Publishing Association
Printed in the United States of America
All rights reserved

Smith, David B., 1955-
    When the Devil makes an offer : how to escape Satan's
plan to trap you / David B. Smith.
        p.   cm.
    ISBN 0-8163-1398-9 (pbk. : alk. paper)
    1. Devil—Controversial literature. 2. Christian life—
Seventh-day Adventist authors. I. Title.
BT981.S57   1997
235' .47—dc21   97-23175
                                                      CIP

00 01 02 03 • 6 5 4 3

Contents

Bad Is Good

Have you ever received a phone call like this one: "Mr. David Smith, I have some wonderful news for you. Mr. David Smith, you've just won a free vacation in Hawaii"? (These people say your name a lot; their manual must dictate that it be included once per sentence.)

I don't know how many free vacations to Hawaii I've won in my life, but I can tell you this: I've never taken a single one of them. Oh, I've been to Hawaii several times . . . and I've had to pay my own way every time.

Now, what's wrong with those so-called "free vacation" phone calls, besides the fact that they call during the eighth inning of deadlocked Dodger games every time? After the "free vacation" part, there's always something else, isn't there?

One company will provide a free hotel room in Hawaii, as long as you book your airline tickets for yourself and your spouse through their company—at $850 a ticket. Or it might be one night free for each night you pay for. And the night you pay for is about two hundred dollars per person double occupancy.

Here's the worst one. You get the free Hawaii vacation as long as you order 25,000 embossed company pens from them. They enclose a sample that reads:

Voce of Prophetic. Have you encountered that prize before?

It reminds me of the swimming pool that humorist Art Buchwald wanted to buy. The swimming pool salesman, a very sincere gentleman, told him it would cost $8,400—complete. This was back in the 1960s, you understand.

Well, that word "complete" was subject to several interpretations. "Complete" didn't include a filter; it didn't include steps to climb out of the pool. It didn't include a diving board. It didn't include the concrete, which cost an extra $500. In fact, it didn't even include the water, which involved another permit costing $250 more. When you got right down to it, the word "complete" only gave you a dirty hole dug out in your backyard.

The crowning blow came when the salesman asked: "Now, how about tree leaves in the pool?"

"I don't *want* any leaves in the pool," the financially choking Mr. Buchwald protested, hoping to save some money.

"We don't put leaves in the pool," the salesman replied cheerfully. "We take them out. You'll want a skimmer for three hundred and twenty bucks more."

Here in these pages we want to take a Bible look at some of the "free" offers being made by the enemy. Our enemy's name is Lucifer. A.K.A. (also known as) Satan. The devil. What is it he's offering us . . . and are his offers really bargains?

You know, you only have to read into the third chapter of Genesis before you find our enemy beginning to do his work. And his work is always the same: **TO MAKE BAD LOOK GOOD**. To make sorrow look like happiness; to make death look like life. And to make the path to destruction look like the freeway to fulfillment.

In verse one, the Bible says: "Now the serpent was more crafty than any of the wild animals the Lord God had made."

Notice that our enemy has put on a serpent suit; he's already in disguise. More about that later. He's crafty. Deception is his Number One weapon; always has been. And he says to Eve: "Did God really say, 'You must not eat from any tree in the garden'?"

Here is Satan's first attempt to drive a separating wedge between God and us. More about that later, too . . . but let's see what happens next.

Eve: "We may eat fruit from the trees in the garden, but God did say, 'You must not eat fruit from the tree that is in the middle of the garden, and you must not touch it, or you will die.' "

Verses four and five are where the enemy really goes in for the kill. Notice now, he uses two key devices: deception and an uncanny ability to make something dangerous and forbidden look good.

"You will not surely die," the serpent said to the woman. You know, that's the first lie ever told in the Bible. The first lie told on this planet. And then the devil goes on: "For God knows that when you eat of it your eyes will be opened, and you will be like God, knowing good and evil."

Well, that's it. Five verses sent this entire planet into the spiral of sin. Those five verses put you where you are today. Sin is something you struggle with; sinful*ness* is your human condition and my human condition. All because Satan was successful in making something look good. He made an offer . . . and Eve took the bait.

"This is good food," the serpent said. "In fact, it's brain food. Come on! Try it! It will open your eyes. You'll know more than you know now. You'll know things God never even intended for you to know. You'll walk on a higher road than He ever thought you could. You'll understand both good and evil. You'll know what's on both sides of the fence . . . and then you can make up your own mind because you are Woman. You're the Queen! You can rule your own life."

Has the desire to know something from the Forbidden Zone ever seemed attractive to you? A lot of times people say, "I just wanted to know what all the fuss was about." What's the buzz with cocaine or crack anyway? What's it feel like, that first drink?

Teenagers wonder to themselves about that first sexual experience. All their friends seem to know. And so they want to know too.

And, of course, the enemy is right there, painting the mysterious unknown in always attractive terms. His brochures are always in four-color, always glossy, always looking good.

Here in Los Angeles we live just close enough to Las Vegas—about three hundred miles—that there are a lot of billboards around town describing the joys of a Nevada vacation. Sometimes you'll see a big dice table with a pair of dice rolling right toward you as you drive along on the freeway.

Notice something the next time you see one. Those dice are almost always rolling out an eleven. A *winning* number. Never a snake-eyes two or a twelve, which means you lose. No, in Vegas people are rolling elevens all day and all night. The winnings are piling up! Why not drive over and cash in?

Well, you're smart enough to realize that this billboard is lying to you. The whole city of Las Vegas is built on a downhill slant. Just like with sin, there's a built-in house percentage that means you're going to come away brokenhearted.

A certain Nevada transaction really typifies the devil's promises to us. A tourist walks up to one of the gaming tables and gives the dealer a hundred-dollar bill. The dealer takes that bill and inserts it into a table slot, a cash box, then gives the player a hundred dollars' worth of chips. But . . . fifteen minutes later, the chips are gone!

Now the house has both the hundred dollars *and* the chips, and the player is broke.

Really, that's the only kind of deal the devil can make with you! There's the promise of fun, of prosperity, of winnings and pretty girls all around. The chips are right there in the rack where you can see them; the billboard promises that you'll win. But when it comes right down to the game itself, the enemy's purpose is to wipe you out. He doesn't give you what he says he'll give you. Really, it's almost appropriate that just about the biggest hotel over there now is called "The Mirage." Think about it.

And here's something else—we can't say we haven't been warned. The Bible is filled with clear, flashing-yellow lights about Satan and his strategies. First Timothy 3 talks about the devil and his traps. In the King James Version, they're called snares. A trap and a snare—both of which employ the trick of dangling something yummy-looking in front of you, hoping you won't see the cage, the bars, the steel jaws of death. It's like a hot-fudge sundae with poison pills in it.

Over in 2 Corinthians 2:11, Paul encourages Christian believers to forgive one another and not allow barriers to build up. For what purpose? ". . . In order that Satan might not outwit us. For we are not unaware of his *schemes*."

In another Bible version it says: ". . . of his *devices*." There's a pattern here, isn't there? The book of John, chapter 8, says that Satan is a liar and the father of lies. You can't trust a word he says.

There's a powerful piece of truth in one of C. S. Lewis' books entitled *Perelandra*. It's Christian science fiction, in a sense, where Lucifer is now on another planet, attempting to deceive the virgin "Eve" of that new world into also sinning.

And the devil, in disguise again, tells this queen about the courage it takes to *dis*obey God! "The way out of obedience is hard," he says, his voice smooth. "It was made hard that only the very great, the very wise, the very courageous should dare to walk in it, to go on—on out of this smallness in which you now live—through the dark wave of His forbidding, into the real life, Deep Life, with all its joy and splendour and hardness."

It sounds so familiar, doesn't it? But this demon in disguise goes on. He actually claims that it was because of the courage of Adam and Eve in disobeying on a faraway planet called Earth that God Himself, Jesus, came down to that world. He tries to suggest that Jesus' coming here to Earth was a benefit, a positive result, of sin.

It's compelling reading, and it gives us keen insights into the silky seductions of the enemy who is still working today. Yes, this is a scary topic—but we don't need to be scared. Satan is a liar, and he's a powerful foe, but he's a defeated foe as well. We can know that even in chapter 1.

Your Friend the Devil

A stand-up comedian once remarked that the ten dumbest, most contradictory words in the English language have got to be: "I am from the government. I'm here to help you." That's the king of all oxymorons.

Now, there are a lot of good men and women who go to Washington with the purpose of helping their constituents back home. Here in Newbury Park, California, where I live, our U.S. representative maintains a field office right in town, and the staff is very helpful. I've called them several times with research questions, and they've gone out of their way to assist me. But it's a common perception that when someone from inside the Beltway in Washington, D.C., comes to you with an offer of "help," you better grab for your purse real fast.

What about the offers from our enemy? Lucifer, the dark prince of this world, often says to us: "I want to help you. I'd like to give you things. I'd like to make you famous. I want to make you happy." But what are his *real* intentions?

Look again at the plain Bible teaching that the devil is a liar. He's the father of lies. Deception is his defining characteristic. In fact, even though we find his first falsehoods in Genesis chapter three—so early in the Bible—the enemy's campaign of lies began even before that. Revelation 12 says: "And there was war in heaven. Michael and his angels fought against the dragon [Satan], and the dragon and his angels fought back. But he was not strong enough, and they lost their place in heaven. The great dragon was hurled down— that ancient serpent [does that sound familiar?]—called the devil, or Satan, who leads the whole world astray. He was hurled to the earth, and his angels with him" (verses 7-9).

Earlier in this same symbol-packed chapter of Revelation, we discover that the dragon's tail sweeps a third of the stars out of the sky and flings them down to the earth. Many Bible prophecy students believe that up in heaven, even before the creation of this world, Lucifer was able to deceive a third of heaven's angels. By lying and deceiving and devices and snares, Satan amassed an army even while he was up in heaven. There couldn't have been much of a war if it was Lucifer against everybody. But the Great Deceiver is exactly that: he does a great job of deceiving.

But now, what are his intentions toward you and me?

You know, when my daughter Kami and I drive down into Los Angeles and go to a Lakers basketball game, I know that Lakers management has one intention toward me. They want my money.

There's nothing wrong with that. But every single facet of organized professional basketball is designed to remove money from my wallet and get it into the NBA's treasury.

There's ticket sales. Parking. Refreshments. Souvenirs. And all through the game, over the PA and on the huge video screens, they plug ice cream sandwiches and tickets to upcoming games and Lakers pennants and Styrofoam "We're Number One" gizmos I can wave in the air. Sure, the Lakers sell us a two-and-a-half hour block of entertainment that's fun. But their intentions are profit-driven.

Let me ask again: what are the devil's intentions toward you?

Here they are: **HE WANTS TO SEE YOU DEAD**. More on that as we go along, but let's face the plain truth. Satan is in the death business. God is the Author of life and happiness; Lucifer is the designing genius behind death and cemeteries and funerals and war and killing and murder and all that goes with it.

And friend, that is what he wants for you! He'd like to get a hold of you—*before* you choose Jesus Christ and eternal life—and snuff your life out. If you've already chosen Jesus as your Savior, he wants to seduce you away from Him. The Bible describes him in 1 Peter 5:8 this way: "Your enemy the devil prowls around like a roaring lion looking for someone to devour."

Now, he doesn't tell you any of this. He says instead, "I'm here to help you. I'm your friend." But the Bible record is clear. Human history is clear. The devil's plan for you ends up in two places: first of all at the cemetery, and then later in the lake of fire that God is preparing for *him*. Satan wants to share that with you.

Look in your own Bible right now and examine Scripture's most revealing episode unmasking Satan's strategy of appearing to be our friend. Here's a quiz question. What's the most hard-hitting temptation story in the whole of Scriptures? Well, that's easy. Lucifer tempting Jesus out in the wilderness. Matthew chapter four or Luke chapter four.

Keep in mind that if Satan's ever going to go all out, it's going to be against Jesus the Son of God. If you want to see all the stops pulled out, then this is where you'll see it. If you want to see the most slippery lies, the most diabolical deceptions, you'll see them when the devil attacks his archrival, his most bitter enemy. Here it is.

In the book of Matthew, the tempter comes to Jesus out in the desert after Christ has been fasting and praying for forty days and nights. And he says to Jesus: "If you are the Son of God, tell these stones to become bread" (verse 3).

Keep in mind one thing, first of all. The devil is in disguise. You know that. He passes himself off as a heavenly angel—not hard for him—and pretends to be Jesus' friend. He's concerned for His well-being. He cares deeply about the hunger of his friend Jesus. "I feel Your pain," he says.

You can almost hear that familiar line from our opening: "I'm here to help You. Jesus, You're so hungry. And You've been praying these forty days. Bless Your heart. God wants You to know that He loves You. And He sent me to tell You, there's bread all around You. . . . in the form of stones. If You're really His Son, then Your time of testing is over. Go ahead and turn these stones into bread and feed Yourself."

It all sounds very nice, doesn't it? Very helpful. Smooth words from a kind friend. Remember that billboard outside a Las Vegas gambling casino? "Come on in! We want you as our special guest. We'll comp you with a suite and a limo and tickets to the floor show. Everyone's a winner here!" And when you get inside, they say, "Go for it! Good luck. We're rooting for you." And here Lucifer says, "Jesus, I'm on Your side. Come on, feed Yourself."

But do you notice a familiar ring to these words that echo all the way back to the Garden of Eden? This tempter says, "*If* you are the Son of God, then turn stones into bread." Back in Genesis 3, we hear a serpent saying, "Did God *really* say not to eat out of this tree?" You can hear a sarcastic little thread of doubt weaving through both of these questions, can't you? "Are you really God? Prove it!" "Does God really mean what He commands? Let's find out."

Four thousand years may separate these two stories, but, I'll tell you, the voice patterns are the same, aren't they? Satan's fingerprints are all over the weapon in both crime scenes.

Let's go to Temptation Number Two. The devil takes Jesus up to the highest point of the temple. "Jump off!" he says. "*If* You're the Son of God, that is. The Bible says God will send angels to catch You, to 'bear You up.' You're in good hands. Etc. Etc."

Here the same strategy continues. "I'm Your friend," the devil tells Christ. "I'm Your partner. Let me help You out here. You want to have a ministry on Earth—and this is the easiest way. Work a miracle or two. Listen, I know these people. A high-wire act from off the temple here, and You'll have all the followers You'll ever need."

What else? This new "friend" quotes Scripture! He knows his Bible! Doesn't that prove that he's a friend sent from heaven?

I guess you and I need to learn that not every person quoting the Bible is automatically your friend. Listen. Just because we quote the Bible on the *Voice of Prophecy* radio program doesn't prove a thing. Not a thing! You need to do what Jesus did: know the Bible for yourself. When you hear a verse read to you over the radio, get out your own copy of God's Word and check it. If a ministry says a verse means this or that, you check for yourself. Study and compare one verse with another. Ask God to guide you and send His Holy Spirit to protect you. Bible quotes don't make a person your friend any more today than they did out there in the wilderness.

Temptation Number Three. And now, finally, the devil lets Jesus see who he really is. He allows himself to be unmasked. He's Lucifer, and he finally stops pretending. Up on the top of the highest mountain, he shows Jesus the world and then says, "OK. Now You know it's me. I'll give You this world the easy way if You'll bow down and worship me."

Now an interesting point. Here we have an unmasked confrontation. The devil against God, one on one. Yet even here, Lucifer pretends to be a friend. "Let me give You what You want," he says. "Don't bother with three-and-a-half years of pain and frustration. Don't bother with Calvary. Don't bother with dying for these people. Work with me here. I'll give You what You came here for . . . and I'll give it to You the easy way."

Let me say it as clearly as I can: DON'T FALL FOR THE FRIENDLY OFFERS OF THE DEVIL! Thank God we have a Saviour who stood up to Satan! Thank God we have a Redeemer who did what He came here to do; He didn't take this shortcut! And thank God we can discover in the example of Jesus how to not be deceived, how to not be beat. Jesus answered Scripture with Scripture! For every twisted Bible quote from Satan, Jesus came back with a better one.

The devil wants to destroy you. Jesus—the victorious Jesus—wants to save you. What more can I say?

Murder or Cards?

A politician walked into a crowded ballroom one day to address a group of voters from one of the ethnic communities in his district. He went up to the microphone and began: "You know, my good friends, in all my years of political life, I've had such admiration for our citizens from Switzerland. The Swiss are, without a doubt, our hardest workers, our most law-abiding, our most industrious people. I'm a big fan of the Swiss people. This is one group that has made a tremendous contribution to society, and I'm just so grateful for my Swiss friends."

One of the politician's aides standing nearby realized that his boss was making a terrible mistake. Someone had given him the wrong information. Slipping up to the podium he whispered to the senator, "Sir, you're addressing the wrong group. These folks are *Germans!*"

Without missing a single syllable, the politician went right on and added: "Yes, the Swiss are wonderful people. But the Germans . . . have always been my favorites!"

Well, that's a politician for you. Some of them manage to get into office with a five-word slogan which they use in every meeting: "Whatever you're for, I'm for." In fact, people complain today that two people representing totally opposite political viewpoints can go into the Oval Office to visit with the president, and both of them will come out later absolutely convinced that the president agrees with *them*.

In this brief volume, we're looking at the tactics and campaign promises of the smoothest, most talented politician in the history of the universe. That's right. The devil is a mastermind at telling you what you want to hear. He'll use whatever speech, whatever promise, whatever temptation is going to be effective with YOU.

One of my favorite books is a 1941 volume by C. S. Lewis entitled *The Screwtape Letters*. In it a senior devil, Screwtape, writes letters of counsel to a nephew, a devil-in-training, named Wormwood, who is assigned to bedevil just one human: YOU. More on that in a moment, but right now let's observe the biblical truth that the prince of darkness does have a plan, a personalized strategy, for you. He's assigned one of his underlings to your case. There's a portfolio that's been carefully put together with your name on it.

That pattern of bit-by-bit slippage, that quiet oozing into danger you sense in your life is the specific work of Satan. That's his campaign strategy! It's not your own doing or the vague gravity of the evil world around us that causes this to happen. The devil has a specific, all-spelled-out, diabolical, computerized plan to ease you into his gun sights.

Here are three words of warning every one of us should mark well. LUCIFER . . . WANTS . . . YOU!! He has a plan to get you into his camp; in fact, he has five billion personalized plans, one for every single citizen of this rebel planet. And his personalized, detailed, itemized, thirty-page strategy report on you takes advantage of every opening, every human weakness or frailty.

Have you ever wondered what Lucifer wants us to think about him? What reputation does he want to have?

There are many people, even Christians, who don't believe in the existence of a real devil. They talk about the Bible's descriptions of the enemy, and they decide that simply refers to our darker side, or man's sinful nature. The *yin* and *yang* of the universe. The *Ormazd* (good) and *Ahriman* (evil) of Persian dualistic philosophy. But a real being called Satan? It's not in their theology.

However, if you and I do allow for the existence of Satan—then how does he react to that? Does he maybe want us not to think he even exists? Does that suit his purpose? Sometimes that's a good wartime strategy: to have the enemy not even know you're there.

It's very clear that Satan is willing for conflicting ideas about him to swirl around. Maybe you remember how back in the early 1970s a book showed up on the bestseller charts entitled *The Exorcist*, by William Peter Blatty. The devil in this story was real. He was in-your-face. He was a being of incredible power and evil. His methods and his workings were plain to see.

Just a few years ago another story was experienced by millions, and this one was a lot softer. It was called *Ghost*. Now, there was no Satan in this story, but there were people who died and then their spirits kind of stayed in the community. There were bad ghosts and there was one good ghost, who had the starring role. But there wasn't a Satan.

Or was there? Let's go again to the Eden Transcripts where Lucifer said to Eve: "If you disobey, you won't *really* die. God said you would, but you won't." And now in an apparently innocent ghost story, a person supposedly dies . . . and he's still around! He dies, but not really! The Bible clearly teaches that the dead don't know anything, that their thoughts perish. But this ghost was right there on the screen, thinking and talking and influencing events and communicating with people.

Now let me ask you. Was Lucifer in this story or not? Absolutely, he was. In a very different form, with a much more subtle and sweet message. But there nonetheless.

Here's my point. Sometimes the devil uses raw power and a show of strength. Just like in warfare, where one side amasses its huge army and even lets the opposing side see it. "Here's what you're going up against." Do you remember some of those old newsreel movies that showed Communist armies parading through the streets of Moscow or Warsaw with tanks and endless rows of soldiers and nuclear missiles? "Here's what you tackle when you mess with us!"

Other times Lucifer holds back. He's in the story, but you don't see him. He lets one of his lies do the work. And a popular Hollywood project makes millions of people think one thing, when the Bible teaches something entirely different!

Here's a third strategy. Lucifer doesn't even mind if we think of him as a joke. Horns and a pitchfork and a little goatee and a red polyester zip-up suit. Do you remember those old Flip Wilson comedy routines: "The devil made me do it"? And we join in with the laugh track. Even preachers tell little jokes about St. Peter at the gate to heaven, and the devil has his kingdom of hell just two blocks down the street. It's a joke! And, you know, the devil doesn't mind a bit.

Do you know why? In all the confusion, most people simply shrug him off. They don't take him seriously! They see news stories about satanism and they say: "Oh, come on. Get real." They see a Hollywood film that features life-after-death experiences which completely contradict the plain teachings in the Bible, and they don't notice the fingerprints of Lucifer on every frame.

Listen, the devil will dress up for you in any suit you want him to. Right now, especially with many young people, he dresses up as himself. He admits it to them: "I'm Satan." And kids who are lonely and hungry for attention and power, and maybe intrigued by something that's mysterious and on the dark, wild side—are attracted by that evil, that power. It's in their music: open worship of the devil. His signs and markings are right on the CD covers.

But not only in appearance, but also in his strategy, Lucifer will use what works. With you and with me. He'll look over his vast arsenal of weapons and choose the one that is going to be effective.

In the book of 2 Thessalonians, chapter 2, we read about the "... work of Satan displayed in all kinds of counterfeit miracles, signs and wonders."

That's a strategy that works amazingly well for him with some believers. They're fooled by displays and emotions.

What about you and me? I've never been tempted to pull a ski mask over my head and rob a bank. I've never been tempted to deal drugs. But as a radio scriptwriter, I'm certainly tempted to overwork. I'm tempted to get impatient over deadlines and time pressures and even innocent mistakes. And, yes, when you're involved in an international radio ministry, it's tempting to forget that this is God's work and His ministry. Someone puts your name on the front cover of a book—and soon it's tempting to have a spirit of pride. I'm thankful that God has a hundred ways to push me off the pedestal, but that's where Satan is going to come after me.

Now to the fictional devil named Screwtape, who is giving advice to his nephew. In chapter twelve, he writes to suggest the effectiveness of tiny distractions, of the most minute, imperceptible movements away from God. Here's what he says:

"You will say that these are very small sins; and doubtless, like all young tempters, you are anxious to be able to report spectacular wickedness. But do remember, the only thing that matters is the extent to which you separate the man from the Enemy. [That's God, of course.] It does not matter how small the sins are, provided that their cumulative effect is to edge the man away from the Light and out into the Nothing."

Now notice what's next. "Murder is no better than cards if cards can do the trick. Indeed the safest road to hell is the gradual one—the gentle slope, soft underfoot, without sudden turnings, without milestones, without signposts."

In fact, this crafty demon suggests: "Keep your man in church. It's better if he stays there, half-asleep. Don't let him realize that the first cracks are happening in the relationship."

WARNING: In the end Lucifer wants to get you away from Jesus Christ. By any means necessary. Maybe on a smooth road, or maybe pushing you right over the cliff. But he wants to get you separated from Jesus. He may hit you with temptations and trials, or he might just let you keep dozing in church every weekend for the rest of your life. Whatever works.

The enemy has a computer file with your name on it. He has a strategy designed to pull you away from God, to destroy your soul. Does that frighten you? It doesn't need to! Because God has a plan too! He has a strategy to protect and shield you.

"Put on the whole armor of God so that you can take your stand against the devil's schemes." Ephesians 6:11. There's a suit of armor for you. There's a personalized plan of protection for you. For every angel of darkness, heaven has twice as many assigned to you.

The devil may try to put on a hundred disguises. But God we know—and He doesn't disguise Himself.

Captain Queeg Was Right

For more than twenty years now, actor Peter Falk has defined the well-known character, "Columbo." This rumpled L.A. police detective with his coffee-stained raincoat never once failed to solve the important homicide cases—and he always managed to do it in just ninety television minutes.

If you've ever seen some of these classic old episodes from the seventies, you remember how so often a small bit of evidence would be the clincher. Most stories involved a man or woman who had carefully planned their crime; these were elaborate schemes to avoid detection. But in every single case, there would be a little, insignificant slice of unnoticed proof that the perpetrator had failed to anticipate or cover up.

In one program it was a carnation in the lapel of a well-known orchestra conductor. Once there was a clock that read backwards in a photo, proving that a certain scene had been staged. In one of the episodes starring Johnny Cash as the bad guy, a set of rental car keys triggered the chain of events that led to his arrest.

But always . . . something small. Never a smoking gun. Never a set of fingerprints. But something little that led to the handcuffs and then the closing credits. Something very small, some little transgression, can lead to eventual ruin. That's true on Columbo television, and friend, it's true in your life and in my life too.

I already mentioned the "roaring lion" warning found in First Peter. But you know, with all due respect, lions don't roar all the time. Sometimes they roar and sometimes they're as still and quiet as a cold winter morning. Sometimes they creep up on their intended victim with such slow, cautious stealth that their approach is never noticed. And sometimes our enemy, the devil, leads us to destruction one inch at a time.

And this is our spiritual challenge for today—to look in the mirror. To notice when that imperceptible drift begins to happen in our lives—and recognize the power behind it.

Here's a bit more of our enemy's plottings, courtesy of C. S. Lewis. Notice the *un*-heavenly advice from "Screwtape" on this very issue: "We know that we have introduced a change of direction in [our subject's] course which is already carrying him out of his orbit around the Enemy [that's God]. But he must be made to imagine that all the choices which have effected this change of course are *trivial* and *revocable*. He must not be allowed to suspect that he is now, however slowly, heading right away from the sun on a line which will carry him into the cold and dark of utmost space."

That's more than a bit scary, isn't it? We think to ourselves, "Aaaah, this is little. It's trivial. It's a revocable thing I'm doing. I can turn around anytime I like . . . but I think I'll drive on just a bit farther."

Every Friday, when I drive Karli to school, there's a faded yellow VW bus parked outside the high school. And I see about ten or so teenagers with their friends before the first class of the day starts. This particular VW must be the unofficial smoking section for Newbury Park High

School, because all ten of them will be lighted up; it's kind of a group thing.

And the once or twice I've gotten up the courage to ask them, "Hey, why are you doing that?"—most of them will say the same thing. "I'm not going to smoke forever. Just right now for the next couple of years. All my friends do, and so I do too. But when I'm a grownup, out on my own, no way. Then I'll quit."

Well, studies show that half of the kids will quit before they enter adult life. However, the other half *won't* . . . and one in five will die prematurely. The odds are as horrible and plain as that.

Just a few weeks ago, a letter came into our Voice of Prophecy offices. Here's what it said. "I'm forty-five years old. I've been smoking since I was fifteen. And today . . . I CAN'T STOP. I simply CAN'T stop."

That was it. Here was a person who took a thirty-year journey with the prince of darkness, starting in 1966, when LBJ was still president and the Beatles were just hitting the charts. A teenage boy smoked one cigarette. What's the big deal about that? Not much, except that now, three decades later, he's a helpless slave, bound more tightly by the nicotine habit than he ever dreamed possible.

"For the want of a nail, the shoe was lost, and then the horse and the whole war." That's Captain Queeg's skimpy paraphrase of the famous essay. In Herman Wouk's book *The Caine Mutiny*, Queeg used the line just days before the mutiny.

If you've ever read the book, you remember that Lieutenant Commander Queeg, who, even as captain of his ship, was slowly going insane there in the thick of World War II, became obsessed that there was a thief aboard his ship. Someone was stealing! Some culprit surely had to have a key to the food box, and he was going to find that key. He had the entire ship searched; he had every man's locker searched; he even had every single man searched. He had to find that key because someone—he was sure of it—had stolen . . . . a quart of strawberries.

When his officers protested to him, "Captain, it's not worth turning an entire ship upside-down, especially during wartime, because of a missing quart of strawberries," that's when Queeg came back with that line. "For the want of a nail, the shoe was lost, and then the horse and finally the war itself."

Now, the telling of this story almost seems to make light of Captain Queeg's assertion. And certainly, here was a man who lost all perspective and was finally issuing orders that stemmed from deep psychological impairment. But underneath the confusion that this fictional Navy officer was experiencing, there was a grain of truth, and it clearly illustrates the devil's favorite strategy, which we discussed in the last chapter.

Queeg was actually right when he told his officers, "Pilfering during wartime, in amounts large or small, is a serious offense." Tell me something. Do you ever commit *little* sins? The kinds we might call "a quart of strawberries"? Now, in this story, the mess boys actually ate the extra strawberries. They didn't steal them from any specific person; there was no need to break-and-enter. They didn't use a gun. And because they were taking them from the general supply, it didn't really even feel like stealing. They were basically just having a second helping—an unauthorized second helping. No one was hurt; the ship didn't go down. The missing strawberries didn't cause them to suffer defeat at the hands of the Japanese fleet. So this was about as little a misdemeanor as you could think of.

And maybe you and I look at our own patterns of "harmless" dishonesty. So we borrow some of the stuff from the office and don't pay it back. The boss asks you a hard question: "Did that report go out yet?" "Sure," you say, even though you really have a couple of pages left to go, and were planning to get it out in the five p.m. shipment. "What's the difference?" you ask yourself. "They'll get it Wednesday either way."

The Bible shares some helpful insights about Satan's domain of "little" sins. In Luke, chapter 16, Jesus Himself made this keen observation: "Whoever can be trusted with very little can also be trusted with much, and whoever is *dishonest* with very little will also be dishonest with much."

Now right here, in the second half of that verse, is something that's a human truth and a Bible truth. Strawberry-stealing, or maybe we could state it generically—sin—is a progressive thing. It always has been progressive, and it always will be progressive. "Small to Big" is always how the tune of sin is played on Satan's Interstate Freeway.

Let's stay with the crew aboard the *Caine*; even though it's a fictional story, it plays very much according to human experience. Here were some well-meaning sailors who dished up extra strawberries for themselves. Sure, it was only *stealing* in the tiniest of senses. But what happened when Captain Queeg, with blood in his eyes, began to whistle for roll call and then question and strip-search all the able-bodied men? Well, they lied about it, of course. They didn't have any choice, they thought. In the frame of mind the captain was in, he might throw them overboard to the sharks or lock them up for a general court martial. So a tiny bit of stealing led to a medium-sized lie, and before the waves had all died down, a major-sized mutiny. First Officer Steve Merrick eventually seized the ship and almost ended up being hanged for his trouble.

Or let's play out the scenario another way. Suppose the guys eat the strawberries . . . and they get away with it. No big deal. Next time out, they "borrow" some of the ship's extra stores, and they make a few bucks selling the surplus on the outside. And there's a term for that, isn't there . . . playing the black market. A few weeks go by, and their more serious customers start demanding this and that rare commodity—which the sailors haven't got. "Well, maybe you can get some if you try real hard," comes the mob-related threat. Before you know it, people aren't just borrowing strawberries; they're involved in flat-out theft, stealing air conditioners and then jeeps and finally aircraft carriers. Well, I'm exaggerating, but you get the point. Our little sins never stay at the "quart of strawberries" level. Someone once observed that it's very, very rare for a young person to go *straight* into heroin as a new habit. Just about always, sin follows a progressive path from mild to medium to more serious to something like murder.

Perhaps you remember the global story in 1995 where a fresh-faced young Londoner named Nicholas Leeson was playing the high-flying financial game of derivative trades on behalf of Barings Bank. Thousands of miles away from home, over in Singapore, this kid was juggling millions of pounds on his computer and living the high life. But then when the market began to go south, he had to make choices.

At first they were smaller choices, smaller coverups, smaller gambles. But as the losses mounted and his derivatives began to completely unravel, the lies grew in quantum leaps. He had to alter documents and try to cover up the paper trail that led to his desk. Finally, in December of 1995, after being extradited from Germany, he pled guilty in a Singapore court of law to the crime of fraud and covering up more than one billion dollars' worth of losses. Notice how Judge Richard Magnus described his progression in crime. Leeson, he said, had "spun a web of deceit." And, of course, a web is spun one thread at a time. That first thread is gossamer-thin. You can hardly see or feel it. But in the end, it had a grip on Nicholas Leeson that will cost this twenty-eight-year-old whiz kid six-and-a-half years in jail.

Well, what does all this mean to us? Let me invite you today, right now, to take stock of your life. I need to do the same. Maybe you see the progression taking place in your life. Look hard; can you see the pattern? Does the enemy have you dipping into things today that five years ago you wouldn't have considered?

Or let me put it to you in a more straightforward way. Why not just look at the small things, the small sins? Look for your own "quart of strawberries." God's Word makes it clear that even those smallest of sins add up. Those single threads are slowly and surely forming a web.

So many times we say to ourselves, "I can handle this." No, you can't. None of us can. And denial is such a dangerous thing. An illicit romance starts out as such a tiny flickering flame. There's a flirtatious remark at work. You say to someone in the hallway, "Boy, you're looking good." And the return response gives you just that imperceptible bit of encouragement. It's innocent, you think. You can handle it. Soon there's the brush of someone's hand against yours, that conversation that strays into the area of your dissatisfactions at home. Your spouse doesn't understand you. And bit by bit, day by day, evening by evening, something small grows into something troublesome, something deadly. We've all heard the stories where someone we thought was so strong, perhaps a Christian minister or gospel musician, ended up doing what once was unthinkable.

Finally, let me add this: don't fight the devil alone! Don't go out to wage the war of little sins by yourself. Tony Evans, in his book *The Victorious Christian Life*, tells the story of pioneer aviator Handley Page, who was flying across desolate territory when he heard a tiny, quiet crunching sound behind him. In the back, where he couldn't reach, a rat was chewing on his food supply. Suddenly frightened, he realized that all the hydraulic lines and control cables were back there too. One misplaced bite could send his plane crashing into the Middle Eastern desert.

Then he remembered a bit of trivia—how rats require more oxygen than even humans do. So he began to climb higher and higher in the air, where the air was painfully thin. In just a few moments, the crunching sound stopped. Hours later, when he landed, he found a large dead rat.

Do you hear the "rat of sin" chewing in your life, Evans asks. And we could ask: the "rat of 'little' sins"? If so, then climb higher! Together with God, soar your plane higher and higher until you starve out those little sins.

"Keep on climbing until the gnawing stops," he writes. "Keep climbing until God brings victory where you did not think victory was possible. Keep climbing until Satan and the old life he dangles before you fall to the floor and die for lack of air."

That's good flying advice, isn't it?

Capturing One Hill at a Time

A dust-covered story from several years ago relates how a man was looking in his attic one afternoon. All at once, he came upon an old, musty, but well-preserved book. Glancing inside the back cover, this man noticed to his horror that it was from the town's public library. What was more to his chagrin was when he saw that the book had been checked out just a little over two *hundred* years ago, back in the late 1700s.

Well, being that he was an honest man, and since that particular library was still operating, he took the book up to the front desk to return it. And you can imagine the response from the librarians when they saw the original check-out date. I can imagine that Jay Leno's writers would have a good time making up jokes about being a slow reader and about the library's policy being two weeks, not two centuries.

But here's the interesting part. One of the librarians calculated what the fine should be for the book coming back in late. Of course, back in the early days it was probably something like two cents a week. But adding up all the late penalties, this man technically owed the public library tens of thousands of dollars for bringing the book back 199 years and 50 weeks past due. The good news:

after brief deliberations, they very graciously agreed to waive the entire fine . . . as long as he promised that the next time he checked out a book, he wouldn't keep it until the year 2197.

Whenever we consider the impact of Lucifer's campaigns, that library fine comes to mind. It builds up! Take a fine of a dollar a week. After two hundred years, even without compound interest, you'd owe more than ten thousand dollars. Apply that thought to that line from the last chapter—"The nail, the shoe, the horse, the war" . . . and it's easy to see how cumulative library fines or cumulative sins can cause us to lose our whole cavalry division.

But here's an additional concern about what we call Satan's "little sins." Something might indeed be a small transgression. In terms of impact or seriousness, maybe it hardly registers a blip on heaven's computer. It's like stealing that quart of strawberries from Commander Queeg's refrigerator on the Caine. But here's the disturbing point. One small sin, even one tiny step in the wrong direction, can put you "out there" where you're suddenly more vulnerable to a more serious temptation.

In C. S. Lewis' book, *Mere Christianity*, he makes what I think is a very compelling argument. See what you think: "Good and evil both increase at compound interest. That is why the little decisions you and I make *every day* are of such infinite importance. The smallest good act today is the capture of a strategic point from which, a few months later, you may be able to go on to victories you never dreamed of" (emphasis supplied).

That's sounds good, doesn't it? But here's the flip side of that same coin. "An apparent trivial indulgence in lust or anger today is the loss of a ridge or railway line or bridgehead from which the enemy may launch an attack otherwise impossible."

What's Lewis saying in this wartime analogy? Inside your fort, maybe you're safe. The enemy can't get you there. But you can step just the smallest bit away from that haven of safety, and suddenly you're in the line of fire. The smallest, most trivial indulgence or bit of compromise today puts you in a place where the devil now can get to you, where before he wasn't able to.

Let me illustrate that with one of the Bible's most tragic and well-known stories: the adultery-murder-coverup soap opera experience of King David.

Here's my question. If you or I—or even Lucifer himself—had gone to that innocent youth, the kid David, out there in the pastures with his sheep, to tempt him with adultery and then murder, how far might we have gotten? Here's a devout young man, a straight-shooting boy with his slingshot and his beautiful God-inspired melodies. And you put the scenario before him: Hey, take this woman, this married woman, and use her. Then plot to kill her husband so that you can cover up your crime.

You know, I get the clear biblical impression that in those early days, back in David's innocence, a temptation like that one would have fallen on deaf ears. "No way!" he would have said. "Never! Not for all the tea in Galilee." In fact, he likely would have responded to this temptation using the same bold words he said to Goliath just before killing him: "I come against you in the name of the Lord Almighty, the God of the armies of Israel. . . . The Lord will deliver me."

But move from the book of 1 Samuel over to 2 Samuel, where David is now the king of Israel. And what happens? There's Bathsheba, bathing on the roof of her house—and King David succumbs to temptation. In fact, he actively plots. He *sends* for Bathsheba. When he finds out she's pregnant, he deliberately tries to cover up his involvement. When that fails, he sends Uriah, her husband, out to the hottest part of the battlefield so that he'll be killed. Adultery—coverup—and murder. Somehow, someway, in the intervening years, something had happened to King David.

Now, what was it that happened? We don't know all those details. We don't know the "back story," as they say in Hollywood. But somehow, one small decision at a time, David edged away from safety and into the danger zone. In battle terms, he lost one little bridge, then a hill over there, and a bunker and a fort and then pretty soon he was standing right out in the open where the enemy's arrows could get to him.

And talk about a beachhead for the enemy! Later on, when David's own son, Amnon, had some moral problems of his own as described in 2 Samuel 13, David pretty much stood by helplessly. Face it: how could he exert much moral influence when he'd been such an abject failure in that very area himself? If he'd even cleared his throat to protest, his son would have told him, "Buzz off, Dad. You did the same thing yourself and you know it." Satan not only infiltrated King David's personal life, but was able to invade the entire royal family—and really, poison the entire kingdom. One sin gave him the toehold he needed.

Maybe you've noticed the same quiet-but-steady march downward in your own life. Perhaps you were raised in a home where the language was always pure and clean. God's name was carefully protected; swear words or obscene remarks were an unthinkable transgression. You and your family followed the Bible counsel to "let your yea be yea and your nay be nay." I mean, you were careful.

Then as a grownup, perhaps in the last ten years or so, television began to very slowly infiltrate your mind with a little bit of mild saltiness. At first those words stuck in your heart like a red-hot dagger. Ouch! Your soul rebelled at hearing that kind of careless talk, that little bit of bath-room humor. But . . . it *was* a funny, cute show. Maybe it was worth the tiny bit of stain on your conscience.

But the following year, you couldn't help but notice that the language was just a bit *more* edgy. The producers were "pushing the envelope," as they say at CBS and Fox. And a couple of friends at work were constantly saying that certain word. Fifty times a day. Pretty soon those words wore a groove in your mind and entered your own vocabu-lary. And you looked in the mirror one morning, or per-haps after church, when God was working on your heart—and you said to the Lord, "How did I get to this point? When did it happen? How did it happen?"

And you look back . . . and maybe you can remember that first moment when you compromised. The TV set stayed on when it should have been turned off. You could have left the room when a cheap, sex-laced story was told at work, but you stayed right there and even kind of forced a laugh. You pretended to go along; in fact, you did go along. And that gave your enemy his first beachhead; it allowed him to plant one of those mountain-climbing hooks in new territory. And he went on from there to capture the whole mountain.

We get so much mail here at the Voice of Prophecy from men and women who find themselves completely locked in an illicit relationship. Or they're imprisoned by some-one who's abusing them—or they're the ones doing the abusing. And they feel totally helpless; in wartime lan-guage, the enemy has them pinned down deep behind his lines. Machine-gun fire is raking the countryside and they see no way of escape.

Well, two points are worth considering. Yes, bit by bit the enemy of this world can trap us. And for many of us, he's done exactly that. But thank God there is rescue. The Bible promises forgiveness whether our sins are still tiny or full-grown and full-blown. Even if Satan has lured us right into the very thick of the battlefield, even if we're up to our eyeballs in his quicksand, God can and will come to our rescue. He's "faithful and just to forgive us," the Bible says. There's no limit to His rescuing power and prowess; there's no war zone where His helicopters can't penetrate.

But the second point is vital as well. God calls us to cooperate with Him, to pay attention to the relationship we have with Him. Yes, He'll forgive small sins and large sins. But let's not presume upon His generosity by carelessly letting those little sins grow to Mount Everest proportions.

In the book of Proverbs, it was ironically the son of King David who made this wise observation—inspired, of course, by heaven: "In *all* your ways acknowledge Him [God]; and He will direct your paths."

In the big things . . . in the little things . . . in all things— let God direct and lead. Why not let Him have it all? Yes, He'll come to rescue and pay that 200-year-old library fine, but how much better to trust Him for the strength to take back your books right when they're due?

Breaking Up the Romance

Here's kind of a naughty question. Have you ever watched an old boyfriend or ex-girlfriend as they went out with the new flame who had replaced you? That certain someone special broke up with you . . . and a couple of weeks later, or maybe even a couple of days later, you see them at Shakey's Pizza Parlor with someone new. And something just burns inside you. What a heartbreaker to watch!

And maybe something inside of you schemed to try to break up that new relationship. What could you do to keep them apart? You've read books about Watergate and Whitewater. Were there any dirty tricks you could play? Maybe you could put sugar in his gas tank so he couldn't go pick her up next Saturday night. Or maybe you could leave a message on her answering machine that would cause her to not like him any more. You know a guy who's good at imitating voices. Maybe it's worth a try.

Well, we hate to admit to thoughts like these, but human jealousy will lead us into all sorts of mischief, won't it?

Here in California, voters recently voted on a statewide initiative that would allow for "open" primaries. Democrats could cross over and vote for Republicans and vice

37

versa. There are arguments on both sides of the question, but one thing is for sure. An open primary does allow for a certain amount of *mischief* in the voting process.

Is it possible that a loyal Democrat, in a year where a Democratic incumbent president is running unopposed, might cross over and vote for the most radical wild-eyed extreme Republican candidate on the ballot? Sure he would! That's what we politely call wreaking havoc upon the enemy. Voters on both sides might have a real interest in promoting, *temporarily* promoting, the least electable candidate the opposition has. You might even send money to help that goofball politician, put one of his bumper stickers on your car, and have his poster in your front yard . . . if you thought that might help break up the opposition's game plan.

Well, what's the spiritual point of all this skulduggery? Imagine that you're the prince of darkness himself: Lucifer. Or maybe one of his evil angels. And there in the Garden of Eden you watch as your enemy, God, creates a beautiful new world and then caps it off with the crowning glory: a man named Adam, and a woman named Eve.

Immediately you hate them, of course. Because God seems to love them so much! In fact, they're His treasure! And you used to be His treasure. You watch with a heart seething with rage as He creates them and caresses them, and then as He speaks those first words of love. You hear God calling them His beloved children. "This is terrible!" you say to yourself. "This makes me sick to watch! What can I do to wreck this friendship?"

Well, it only gets worse. It's Friday afternoon by now, and the next thing you hear God announce is that He's going to spend the whole next day with Adam and Eve. He's going to fellowship with them and nurture this virgin friendship. It's going to be a glorious time of joy and laughter and walks through Eden and hours of worship and celebration. This new thing called Sabbath will be filled with singing and with happiness and love. And for a whole twenty-four hours, not just this week, but every week, God's going to come back to this tiny planet and spend the whole day with Adam and Eve and with all their kids and grandkids.

And you're the enemy watching from behind the nearest bush. "This is a nightmare!" you say to yourself and to all the others in your army. "If these people cozy up with God for a special day of joy each week, we're finished before we start! Their love will grow and flourish . . . and we'll waste away here on the sidelines."

So then you and your team draw up your battle plans. And this new creation called "The Sabbath" is one of the highest things on your to do list. Somehow you've got to attack this business of the seventh day of rest. Either head-on, or from the side, or by subterfuge and dirty tricks; Lucifer and Company are hell-bent, no pun intended, on getting rid of the whole concept of Sabbath rest and fellowship between heaven and earth.

Does that make sense? Sometimes it's helpful to think with the mind of the opposition, isn't it? "Know your enemy" . . . that's the old battle slogan. And from a jilted lover's perspective, if you knew that your "ex" was spending a whole day a week doing nothing but basking in the love of someone new, wouldn't you start subscribing to *Soldier of Fortune* magazine and begin thinking of strategies?

Let's just look at the record of history, because the War Chronicles are right there for our examination. The Sabbath, this wonderful haven of communication and fellowship, was brought into existence in Genesis, chapter 2. It's mentioned again in Exodus 16. But by the time we get to Exodus 20, it's clear that the Sabbath has largely been forgotten. It never ceased to exist—but it certainly was

buried and forgotten. Long centuries of slavery in Egypt
will tend to do that; the confusion of sin and a flood and a
tower of Babel contributed as well. In a fascinating book
exploring this very concept, entitled *A Pause For Peace*,
author Clifford Goldstein notes with colorful insight: "If,
in one generation, American TV can go from censoring
Elvis's jiggling hips to allowing Madonna to parade around
in nothing but a black teddy—imagine what two centuries among the idols, pyramids, and gods of Egypt did to
the Jews!"

So our enemy has used the strategy of just plain forgetting. No wonder the Fourth Commandment begins by saying: "*Remember* the Sabbath day to keep it holy."

But Lucifer, prince of lies and lapsed memories, had
other campaign tricks. He could pervert the Sabbath, make
it wearisome and a burden to keep. He could quietly move
upon men to bury God's special day with a million tiny
rules and regulations and codes and codicils. Instead of
the Sabbath being a delight, as it's described in Isaiah 58,
he could pile on the rules until it became the worst day of
the week.

And you know, by the time Jesus Christ our Saviour
arrived on our planet, Plan B had pretty much worked to
perfection. The Sabbath was there, all right. Nobody in
Israel was forgetting the Sabbath; no way. You couldn't
forget the Sabbath with the nine million billboards all
around Jerusalem posting the restrictions. As Clifford
Goldstein points out in his book, two of the Jewish
tractates in the Talmud, *Shabbath* and *Erubin*, deal spe-
cifically with the Sabbath and all the minutiae that now
surrounded it. There were more rules than you could read,
let alone observe.

And the Sabbath being a delight? Not a chance. All the
innocent joy, the happy shrieks of children playing by a
mountain stream, the savoring of a love relationship with

God . . . all that was gone. Chalk up one more for the enemy.

How about today?

Do you know something? Together we praise God for the Cross of Calvary, don't we? Every Christian around the world owes his or her spiritual life to that magnificent Friday at Golgotha and the resurrected Christ. Let me say plainly: nothing we can ever do, no amount of obedience or commandment keeping can qualify us for heaven. Calvary qualifies us for heaven . . . period. That's bedrock Christian truth, and here at the Voice of Prophecy, we hold unswervingly to that gospel pillar.

But I have to openly tell you something else. I truly believe it's a strategy of the devil if we *then* come to the conclusion that of all the Ten Commandments, the fourth one is the only one that grateful Christians in the twentieth century should no longer keep. "Oh, we're not bound by that commandment any longer," some say. They obey the law of love as summarized by Christ in the New Testament in places like Mark 12. "Love God and love your fellow man." Which, of course, continues to cover beautifully Commandments One through Three and Five through Ten. But as interpreted that way, somehow the gift of the Sabbath . . . is lost. The restoring power of that day, that full, wonderful, beautiful, complete day of fellowship with our King Jesus and with our God is lost.

Now, however you want to interpret Scripture, and no matter how you choose to read and apply the gospel message to your own life, this much is true: the disappearance of the Sabbath is always a victory for the enemy. If he steals from you that day, that sacred time of hand-in-hand, heart-to-heart fellowship with God, that's victory. Every time, it's victory for the enemy. He delights and celebrates whenever we forget the Sabbath, or choke it with rules, or even if we read into our own Bibles any interpretation that erases the Sabbath from Christian life.

That's why I'm so glad that Christians in many different denominations are being seized with a renewed conviction on this matter. "Wait a minute!" my Baptist friends are saying, and my charismatic brothers and sisters, and my business associates who are active in the Methodist denomination, and even my fellow Seventh-day Adventists who may have fallen into the trap of keeping a Sabbath but losing the joy of the experience. "Something's been lost here! The devil's won a battle, but let's not let him win the war."

You know, six thousand years ago God pursued His children Adam and Eve like a jealous lover. The Sabbath was His gift to them because He loved them so much; He craved their friendship and their fellowship.

He's just the same today, you know. He feels exactly that way about you. Right now. What do you think about that?

Time-Travel Theology

In a story entitled *Time After Time*, the old time-travel writer, H. G. Wells, has traveled out of the nineteenth century and into 1979 San Francisco, and is trying to prevent Jack the Ripper from committing yet another terrible crime.

Now, because of this time-traveling miracle, Wells knows all about the future murder. He knows where and when and how it will take place. He's determined to prevent it; he thinks he can alter a future event. But as he's traveling to the scene of the yet-to-be-committed crime, suddenly a car tire goes flat. And the crime, which he *knew* was going to happen . . . happens. Things were fixed in destiny; he couldn't change them.

Probably a more well-known Hollywood sci-fi project along a similar theme was the old *Back to the Future* trilogy, where a kid named Marty McFly, played by Michael J. Fox, travels into the past and the future via a DeLorean time machine. And even there you see this thread where sometimes the future could be changed, the so-called space-time continuum . . . and sometimes it couldn't be changed. He'd try to prevent something terrible from happening, because he *knows* it's about to, and he runs out of gas.

Probably the most wrenching—and certainly cheapest—

of such imaginary adventures is an old TV program where a time traveler determined to travel back to a Friday in Dallas, November 22, 1963 . . . and try to prevent John F. Kennedy from being assassinated. So he went back in time to, let's say, 12:15 in the afternoon there in Dallas. But you know, every single time, something would go wrong. A flat tire. Traffic. The elevator wouldn't work at the Texas Book Depository. And the hard thing was that the actor playing Kennedy kept getting killed over and over and over again. That assassination was a fixed event that could not be erased out of history.

Well, it's maybe an interesting bit of fantasy. But I find in this odd kind of story a powerful Bible truth. And here it is: GOD IS GOING TO WIN! That is a fixed truth. It can't be changed; it can't be overcome; it can't be undone. The fact of God's victory is concrete truth that you can hold onto today.

There are things about the war between Christ and His enemy, Satan, that are still in the future. They haven't happened yet. And one might think that those future events are subject to alteration. A great heroic effort, or a demonic one, could overturn them—you would think.

And you couple that suggestion with the obvious truth that the Church of Christ is struggling here on earth. The devil is winning wars all over the place. Things are shaky for the people of God.

And yet the Bible promises about ultimate victory are absolute, unshakable, unchangeable truth.

In the book of Revelation, especially starting in chapter 19, we find ringing promises that tell us God simply IS NOT going to lose. Chapter 19 describes the Rider on the White Horse, Jesus Christ. And He's followed by the armies of heaven. They don't come down here to lose; they come down here to win.

Revelation 20:10 describes the final battle: Armageddon. What happens? God wins, the devil loses. Then in chapters 21 and 22, more descriptions of the victory, not only for God, but for God's people. Those who are allied with God will share in His victory. "Now the dwelling of God is *with men*, and He will live with them. They will be His people, and God Himself will be with them and be their God. He will wipe every tear from their eyes. There will be no more death or mourning or crying or pain, for the old order of things has passed away"(Revelation 21:3, 4).

Let me make an assertion—and I hope this doesn't sound flip or casual. But I almost see God's enemy in terms of that kid driving around helplessly in that time-traveling DeLorean. No matter where he is in the space-time continuum, no matter what he tries to do, the devil just keeps losing. He's the Flat-Tire King of all time. Every strategy he tries backfires! In fact, even when he wins . . . he loses.

Let's go to the Garden of Eden. And we see the devil's DeLorean parked outside the front gate behind a bush. And he wins a little battle: Adam and Eve sin and become his captives.

Then what? Not one chapter later, a Redeemer is promised. Jesus will win them back. And the serpent's victory turns into defeat.

Travel down a couple of thousand years. There's that same DeLorean parked on a sand dune by the Red Sea. The Children of Israel are trapped. Mountains all around, the sea's in front of them, the whole Egyptian army's behind them and coming on strong. The devil can't lose this time! Except that God opens up the Red Sea, then closes it just in time to swallow up the whole enemy army. Another blockbuster loss.

Now we move to Jesus in that Garden of Gethsemane, and then on the Cross of Calvary. This looks like the biggest enemy win of all history. Jesus is dead in the tomb; the war's over. Satan has won! But it turns out not to be. The resurrected Son of God comes out of the tomb. Darkness turns into light. Tragedy becomes triumph. And all Satan can do is watch in bitter frustration from the sidelines as his biggest campaign fails. No matter what he tries, God simply will not be beat.

In the early Christian church, God's followers are persecuted and tortured and killed. The battlefield is covered with blood. But for every Christian soldier who falls, a hundred new ones spring up to take his or her place. The blood of those martyrs waters the meadows of the Dark Ages, and the church actually grows and thrives. Satan . . . simply . . . can't . . . win.

It gets to be the year 1517. The medieval church is locked in heresy and superstition; the enemy has managed to infiltrate it with pagan practices and false teachings. He's on the verge of a huge triumph. But then October 31 comes around and a monk named Martin Luther goes up to the church there in Wittenberg and nails something called "The 95 Theses" to the door. The Protestant Reformation is born; the pure Christian church is revived. Satan was *so close* . . . and he loses again.

And even now, the same scenario is being played out again. Maybe it's happening in your life. Lucifer is attacking you; he's pelting you with temptations and discouragement. Maybe he's hitting you with the temptation to seek a divorce or a habit you just can't break. He's so close to victory, because you're about ready to give up.

But you know something? He pushes you just a little bit too far. His hatred overshadows his wisdom and his craftiness. He's so close to enslaving you for good, but that last temptation, that last trial is just one too many. And you're so discouraged, so in despair, that the devil actually drives you down *onto your knees*. That's right! He pushes you to your knees—and you cry out, "Jesus, save me!"

And I've seen this time after time; in fact, I've experienced it in my own life! The devil doesn't know when to quit, and he sabotages his own campaigns! He ends up losing in the very projects he starts. He steps on his own land mines.

I want to tell you *half* of my favorite expression. Just half . . . and here it is. "SATAN IS MIGHTY."

Would you agree with that? He IS! He's a mighty foe! First Peter describes him as an enemy, an adversary, a roaring lion capable of devouring us. He's a dangerous enemy; he's not to be trifled with. At the Voice of Prophecy radio ministry we consider Lucifer to be a very real being, a tangible enemy, a formidable foe. He's the prince of darkness. Let me say again: SATAN IS MIGHTY.

But praise God . . . because that's only HALF of my favorite saying. And I know you know what the entire saying is: SATAN IS MIGHTY . . . BUT JESUS IS **ALMIGHTY**!!

That's right! Wherever you are, know this to be true. Satan is mighty. He absolutely is. But Jesus Christ is almighty. And when it comes to war, "almighty" beats "mighty" every single time.

I don't know if you've ever played that old kid's card game, ironically called "War." You pull out a card and then your opponent pulls one out—and the higher card wins. And every time Satan pulls out a six, God has a seven. Satan gets a king, and God has an ace. Every time! He doesn't lose!

In one of our favorite Voice of Prophecy resource books, *The Knowledge of the Holy*, by A. W. Tozer, he points out that the English Bible uses the word *almighty* fifty-six times. And do you know something? All fifty-six are in reference to God. Not to us; not to a great king like David

or Solomon. Not to the twelve disciples. And not to the
devil! The devil is mighty, but God is almighty. He doesn't
ever lose. No matter where you park your DeLorean and
get out, you see God winning again.

Lucifer Looking
for Company

So what do you do when you *know* you're going to lose?
I'll get mail for saying it, but I guess we could ask
the Buffalo Bills that question. Along around the third
quarter, it happened four years in a row. The Big
Game—the Super Bowl—and in '91, '92, '93, and '94,
the Buffalo Bills and Coach Marv Levy could just feel it
slipping away.

And finally you get to the point where, mathematically,
you can't win. Two minutes left in the game and you're
down by four touchdowns. You simply cannot win.

Or a presidential candidate comes down to the evening
before the election, and he's down in public opinion polls
by fifteen points. Now, Harry Truman pulled out that big
win over Dewey in 1948, but since then polls have been
pretty accurate. Those CNN/Time statistics tell you:
"You're *going* to lose!"

That's the position our enemy, Lucifer, finds himself in
today. He's going to lose! That's as clear a headline as we
can find in this universe. For six thousand years a war
has been going on . . . but the outcome of that war is known.
God is going to win; the devil is going to lose.

What, then, is his reaction? And what does it have to
do with you and me?

Our Bibles describe Lucifer's beginnings. You can find his story in Isaiah 14:12-14: "How you have fallen from heaven, O morning star, son of the dawn! You have been cast down to the earth, you who once laid low the nations! You said in your heart, 'I will ascend to heaven; I will raise my throne above the stars of God; I will sit enthroned on the mount of assembly, on the utmost heights of the sacred mountain. I will ascend above the tops of the clouds; I will make myself like the Most High.' "

That's where our enemy comes from. He used to be an unfallen being; now he's a fallen being. And ever since Calvary, he's been a *defeated* fallen being . . . and he knows it. He's aware that he can't win.

In another book entitled *Watching the War*, I once suggested that perhaps there was a point where Lucifer actually believed in his own campaign. He really believed God was unfair; maybe he honestly thought he could set up a rival government that was better and more conducive to freedom and happiness and personal fulfillment.

But you know, even by the first few chapters in the book of Genesis, as Satan looked around at the fruits of sin—death and hatred and bitterness and endless betrayals—even he had to know in his heart that his campaign was a failed one. Things were spinning out of even his control; he could see that his confused government was fatally flawed; it contained an element of pure wrongness.

But people who are wrong sometimes win! In World War II, the Nazis nearly triumphed. Could evil win here? Until Calvary, that was an open question.

But no more. The book of Revelation clearly spells out Lucifer's end. Chapter 20 describes the lake of fire where the enemy of this universe will meet his end.

Let me ask again: what do you do when you *know*

you're going to lose?

If you're a politician, you might bluff. "We can still pull it out," you tell the TV cameras, hoping the perspiration on your forehead doesn't show. "Polls don't vote; people do. There's going to be a big surprise tomorrow. We're gunning for an upset!" You try to put a positive "spin" on the situation.

If you're a football player, you just keep running the ball until the final gun sounds. You keep knocking heads; in fact, maybe you knock heads a little bit harder when you know your cause is lost.

How about the devil? Who does he take out his frustration on?

Earlier we took a peek into C. S. Lewis' marvelous book *The Screwtape Letters*. Now, a devil really didn't write these letters, but they certainly have an authentic ring to me. And in a couple passages, the enemy's frustration shows through. He writes about all the joys and pleasures that God has created for His followers. Listen: "Never forget that when we [Satan and his angels] are dealing with any pleasure in its healthy and normal and satisfying form, we are, in a sense, on the Enemy's [God's] ground. I know we have won many a soul through pleasure. All the same, it is His invention, not ours. He made the pleasures: all our research so far has not enabled us to produce one."

Later in the book this senior devil complains again about God's natural advantages: "Out at sea, out in God's sea, there is pleasure, and more pleasure. He makes no secret of it; at His right hand are 'pleasures for evermore.' He has filled His world full of pleasures. There are things for humans to do all day long without His minding in the least—sleeping, washing, eating, drinking, making love, playing, praying, working. Everything has to be *twisted* before it's any use to us. We fight under cruel disadvantages. Nothing is naturally on our side."

Well, some of C. S. Lewis's writing is amusing, but do you catch the anger there? "We fight at such a disadvantage," he complains. "And we're going to lose!" Even the demons know that God is right and they are wrong and that destruction is going to be their fate.

When we consider the offers of the enemy, C. S. Lewis is right—Lucifer doesn't have a single permanent thing he can offer you. Except one: destruction. That's it.

And all the demons' greatest anger comes from the fact that God is intending to save *you*. Think about it. These are creatures filled with sin. And you're a creature filled with sin. And yet, God has announced to the universe that He has a plan to save you. He's going to take you to heaven! Give you eternal life! You don't deserve it any more than the devils of hell do, but He's going to do it anyway.

How, then, does Lucifer feel about you and about me? He hates us with every fiber of his being. His entire army is seething with resentment and hatred over what God intends to do with *us*.

I know you've heard this expression: "Misery loves company." I saw that cliché dramatically played out a few years ago.

The San Francisco Giants were about to clinch the National League Western Division. There were just six games left in the season, and they were six games ahead of their nearest competitors.

Now, my beloved Dodgers were out of it. (Actually, I kind of hated them that year.) They were a million games back. And all the Giants had to do was beat the Dodgers *one time*. One game out of three. Just one victory would mean that they'd mathematically lock up the championship. Their so-called "magic number" was one.

No, the Dodgers weren't going anywhere. They were

wallowing in the misery of the cellar. But they decided that if they couldn't be division champs, at least the Giants weren't going to celebrate at Dodger Stadium. The enemy wasn't going to win that clinching game in their park.

So the last-place Dodgers won that first game. They won the second game. And in the third game, they jumped out to a lead and held on.

It came down to the last few innings. And the fans, sensing that this was kind of a special moment, began an interesting two-word chant.

"NOT HERE! NOT HERE!"

Soon it was rocking through Dodger Stadium. "NOT HERE!" In essence they were saying: "Okay, so we're losers. But tonight you Giants are losers too. You may win later, but you're not going to drink champagne in our stadium. No way!"

So . . . the devil's going to be destroyed. And in his heart he has a burning, indescribable hatred for God—and for all of God's trophies. Because God loves you, the devil hates you. Because God wants to see you in heaven, he'd like to see you in that lake of fire that's going to be created for him. It's his lake of fire, but he wants to share it with you. Misery loves company.

I read a beautiful, old-fashioned description of this war, this boiling-over resentment of Lucifer's. This comes from an old religion magazine dated 1886. Here's what it says:

> This is the argument that Satan employs concerning God's people in all ages. He pleads their sinfulness as the reason why Christ's restraining power should not hold him back from exercising his cruelty upon them to its fullest extent. But to the accuser of His people the Saviour says, 'The Lord rebuke thee, O Satan. Is

not this a brand plucked out of the fire? Have I
not thrust My own hand into the fire to gather
this brand from the burning?"

You know, I like that. God looks down at Lucifer, who is
trembling with rage, shaking in his desire to destroy you
and me. And God, very calmly, but with quiet strength,
says simply: "No. These are the treasures I've plucked out
of the fire. *These* I am saving. End of discussion."

Satan Overreaches Himself

This chapter originally came from a "Friday" radio broadcast . . . and it seems like we're always glad when Friday rolls around.

Especially at the Voice of Prophecy, it seems like Friday is always the day when our week-long radio script turns the corner . . . and we discover God's good news. Recently we had a week of programs entitled *A Kid Named Joe*. And if you were with us, you remember how the Bible story of Joseph was a long saga of heartache and repeated disappointments—until we got to Friday. On Friday everything worked itself out.

And I guess when you consider that Friday is the day we come to Calvary and the cross of Christ, it's not surprising that we find good news on Friday. Our redemption always happens on Friday.

In these chapters, we've been exploring the offers coming from the enemy. Those letter bombs dropped from the enemy airplanes flying over our war zone, promising us all sorts of good things if we'd follow Lucifer.

The devil is a liar. We *know* that. He's got a track record of deception. He'll use any device, any snare, that he can come up with in order to lure you into his net. And what he has in mind for you is death. That's something we know.

Lucifer's blueprint for your life ends up in the cemetery and then the lake of fire.

For a while, some of his posters look pretty good. His lies paint "bad" as "good." Recently a publisher mailed me a gift book as an entry for a religious award. I won't tell you the title, but it was all about "a compelling vision of the afterlife." The writer was a kind of New Age guide, who described in vivid detail the peaceful new level of life, of existence, experienced by people who have died. It was beautiful! It was fulfilling! Our mothers and fathers and even children who tragically have been killed, she said, are now happy in a new plane of existence. Everything is wonderful there. It's all glowing light and harmony.

There's only one problem. If you read God's Word, you find out that everything she said is a lie. It simply isn't true. The Bible paints no such picture.

Especially dangerous about a lie like this one is how it glosses over the need to enter into a personal trust relationship with Jesus Christ. The Bible clearly states: "Believe in the Lord Jesus and you will be saved" (Acts 16:31).

And Jesus said, "*I* am the way, the truth, and the life. No one comes to the Father except through Me." But a book like this comes along and says, "Oh no. *Everybody* goes to the grassy hill where the soft sunlight is bathing the surroundings. Everybody enters into eternal life regardless of whether or not they paid any attention to the claims of Christ. Believers and unbelievers alike are up in Paradise."

Well, what are you going to believe? Attractive lies or the life-saving true warnings in the Word of God?

It's tragically true that sometimes, even when we know we're being lied to, we can't resist sin. I think of the lies told to us by cigarette companies. Smoking will give you an aura of sophistication, they suggest. It's an "adult" habit for "discerning" people to decide for themselves.

Back in 1995, I wrote a tongue-in-cheek radio spot where a tobacco company representative is on the witness stand, and he's asked whether or not his company wants kids to smoke. Here's the fictional answer we had him give:

"Oh, absolutely not. You see, smoking is an adult habit. Always has been. This is a decision that's very sexy, very glamorous . . . I mean, you look good when you smoke. Everybody knows that. And that kind of raw sex appeal is just too much for kids to handle. You light up one of our full-flavor, low-tar cigarettes and then stand there outside the mall with the smoke just curling out like that, maybe you're wearing a black tank top—and the opposite sex is going to be all over you. And kids . . . they aren't ready to withstand that kind of hard-edged sex-laced pressure. And so we in the tobacco companies are on the record saying that we don't want innocent kids to have to go through this type of hot-pounding adult experience. It's too soon, kids. This is still forbidden fruit; you're going to have to wait a little longer."

Yeah! Smoking is so cool! Look how cool Joe Camel is . . . and hundreds of thousands of kids are trying real hard to be as cool as the Party Animal himself.

But I'll tell you something. For every kid who's fooled by the four-color ads and the Marlboro sports gear, there are ten smokers who *know* they're being lied to. They know cigarettes are a killer. They know they're being suckered. But they simply can't help themselves. They feel helpless to resist.

Sometimes people are caught in the trap of adultery. They know they're being lied to. They know there's heartache on the other side of that one-night encounter. They hear a slow-dance bluesy song on the radio: "Help me make it through the night." "It can't be wrong when it feels so right." And they know in their hearts it's a lie; they know they're risking a lot, maybe even their life, with the threat of AIDS lurking out there now. But sin is just too powerful; they're a slave to its seductive hold on them.

Listen, sin is a delusional thing. You're lied to . . . and sometimes you don't know it, sometimes you DO know it—and you still do it. Knowing the glass contains poison, you drink from it anyway.

But it's Friday. The power of the Cross is being offered to you right now because it's Friday. Escape from the traps of Lucifer is possible for you right now.

I want to add one more bit of wonderful Friday good news. Sin is so deceptive in its power that it even deludes and destroys its very source. That's right. Satan himself, our enemy, is *self-deceived*.

Earlier we considered how Satan would do well to leave some people alone—people who are half-asleep in their Christianity and dozing in the church. People who are trying to live a good life, an obedient, upright life without a relationship with Jesus.

Satan would be smart to leave people like that alone. And according to *The Screwtape Letters*, he really plans to leave them alone. But then something amazing happens.

Morris Venden, in his book *To Know God: A Five-Day Plan*, describes how sometimes when a person decides to have a relationship with Jesus Christ and spend time each day getting to know Him . . . boy, the roof caves in! Everything goes wrong! Lucifer and two thousand of his hand-picked evil angel troops swoop down and just blast that baby Christian. Temptations and discouragement and traffic jams and flat tires and everything.

So sometimes that new believer says, "This is terrible! Spending time getting to know God doesn't work. I never sinned so much in my life!" And the next morning they sleep in. They skip their time of Bible study and prayer.

So what does a smart Lucifer do then? He leaves that person alone, Venden writes. And so now he has a good day. Everything goes great. He or she even seems more obedient, because there are fewer temptations. The natural reaction? "I guess I'm doing better this way. I don't need to be a Christian."

In fact, Venden describes how a student once came up to him and said, "You know, I quit being a Christian two weeks ago, and I haven't sinned since!" And he writes: "Often we find that at the point we scrap the relationship with Christ, things apparently go better. Our problems seem to cease."

Ah . . . but what happens next? This is what's so interesting. Venden goes on: "Right there you would think that the devil would be smart enough to leave well enough alone. But as number one sinner in the universe, Satan has a remarkable lack of control. He goes along for a couple of weeks leaving me alone, and he has me, because I'm not seeking God, not praying, not into the Word of God."

Now comes the punchline: "But then he comes at me again—just for fun this time. He's not happy to see a person lost; he'd like to have him in the gutter as well. So when he comes in after a week or two and brings more trouble, it drives me to my knees. We say, 'I guess I do need this experience with God, after all.' "

Venden concludes by sharing his own personal testimony: "If the devil had been smart enough, he would have left some of us alone, and he would have had us a long time ago. But he continued to needle us until we were driven to God *permanently*. God can bring some of the devil's maneuvers out to His own glory, can't He?"

You know, Lucifer, the father of lies, ends up defeated by his own self-deceptions. How many of us are safely in God's hands today because Satan just wasn't smart enough to leave us alone? He kept pushing us and tormenting us and tempting us until he drove us right into the arms of Jesus!

I said at the very outset—Satan is clever. He's a liar . . . and a good one. He's powerful and masterful and determined to take you and me down with him.

But remember: Satan is mighty; Jesus is ALmighty. Satan has a plan; Jesus has a better plan. When Satan reminds you about your past, you remind him about his future.

And his future is one you don't have to have any part in . . . because it's Friday. Today's our Calvary moment, our time of rescue.

Yes, friend, Jesus keeps His promises. And Jesus has promised to save you. That's right, I mean *you*. Jesus means *you*, wherever you are reading these last words. "Whosoever will, may come," He said. And He said it with *you* in mind.